Tools That Help Me

Adam Schaefer

Rourke
Publishing LLC
Vero Beach, Florida 32964

www.rourkepublishing.com

PHOTO CREDITS: © Andres Balcazar: cover; © Kary Nieuwenhuis: page 5; © Andres Balcazar: page 7; © Tim Pohl: page 11; © Jan Ellen Ball: page 13; © Holly Kuchera: page 15; © Andres Balcazar: page 17; © Sharon Dominick: page 19; © Ericsphotography: page 21

Editor: Robert Stengard-Olliges
Consulting Editor: Luana Mitten

Cover design by Nicola Stratford

Library of Congress Cataloging-in-Publication Data

Schaefer, Adam.
  Tools that help me / A.R. Schaefer.
       p. cm. -- (The world around me)
  ISBN 1-59515-996-7 (Hardcover)
  ISBN 1-59515-968-1 (Paperback)
  1. People with disabilities--Orientation and mobility--Juvenile
literature. 2. People with disabilities--Transportation--Juvenile
literature. 3. People with disabilities--Services for--Juvenile literature.
I. Title.
  HV3001.A4S33 2007
  681'.761--dc22
                                        2006022161

Printed in the USA

CG/CG

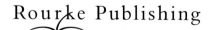

Rourke Publishing

www.rourkepublishing.com – sales@rourkepublishing.com
Post Office Box 3328, Vero Beach, FL 32964

Table of Contents

Introduction

Everyone uses tools every day. If we need to cross a busy street we wait for the signal to see if it's safe to cross. Crosswalk signals are a helpful tool.

STOP

GO

Tools for People Who Can't See

Some tools are made especially for people who have a **disability**. A helpful tool for someone who can't see is a white cane. When a person who is **blind** walks on a busy sidewalk, they move the cane from side to side to make sure nothing is in their path.

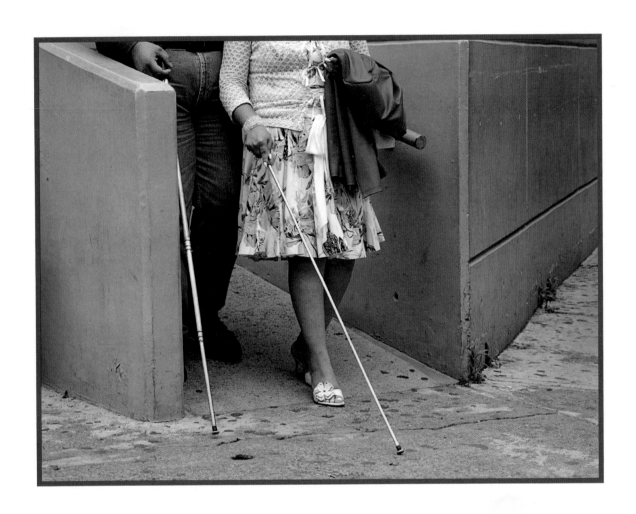

Have you ever seen rows of bumps at the end of a sidewalk? These bumps are another helpful tool for people who can't see. They can feel the bumps with their feet to learn where the sidewalk ends and the street begins.

Some books have a pattern of bumps on them instead of words. These bumps are **Braille**. Braille is a tool that helps people who are blind read with their fingers. They run their fingers over the patterns of bumps that stand for letters and numbers.

Tools for People Who Can't Hear

A helpful tool for someone who has trouble hearing is a hearing aide. Hearing aides make sounds louder and clearer.

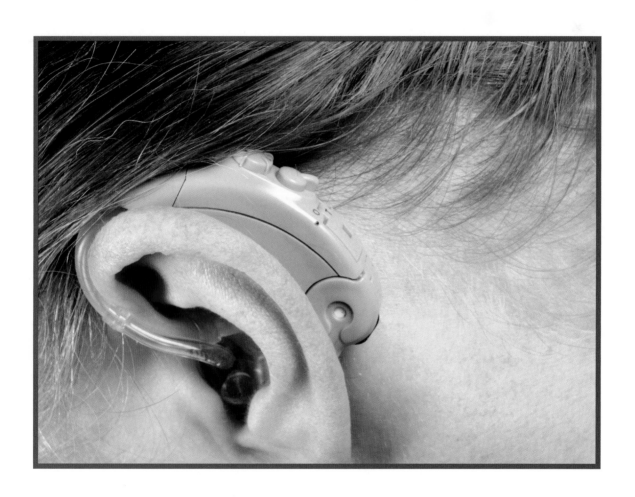

13

Many people who can't hear or speak communicate using sign language. **Sign language** is a tool like Braille. Instead of bumps for letters, hand motions form words or ideas.

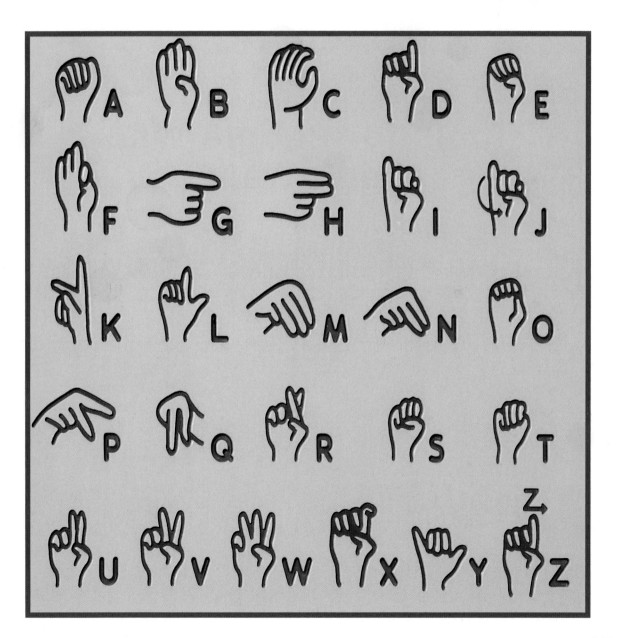

Tools for People Who Can't Walk

Some people need help walking or can't walk at all. A walker or wheelchair is a helpful tool for them to move from place to place.

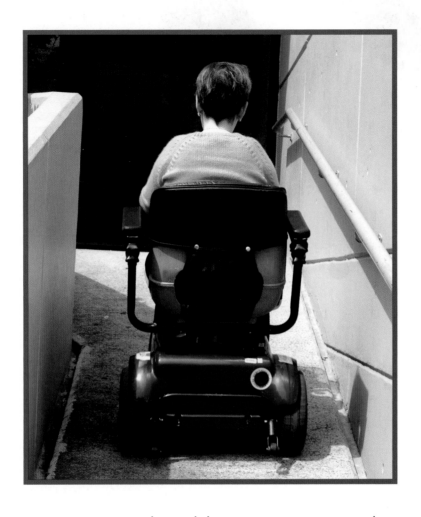

Have you ever wondered how someone who uses a wheelchair or a walker goes up and down steps? Ramps help people using wheelchairs and walkers get over curbs and up and down stairs.

Ramps also allow kids in wheel chairs to play at playgrounds and parks. We call places with ramps for wheelchairs "Handicap Accessible."

19

Wheelchairs are tools that help people who can't walk go as many places and do as many things as they can. Some people play sports or race in wheelchairs.

These are just a few of the tools people with
disabilities find helpful. Can you think of any other tools
in your community that help people with disabilities?

Glossary

blind (BLINDE) — very limited or no sense of sight

Braille (BRAYL) — system of writing and printing for the blind based on raised dots

disability (diss uh BIL i tee) — refers to the social effects of physical or mental impairment

sign language (SINE LANG gwij) — uses hand signals to communicate rather than sounds

Index

Further Reading

Esherick, Joan. *Breaking Down Barriers : Youth with Physical Challenges.* Mason Crest Publishers, 2004.

Websites To Visit

http://www.nbp.org/ic/nbp/cbbc/index.html

http://www.therapyanimals.org/read/index.php

http://www.caninesforkids.org/

About The Author

A.R. Schaefer has written more than 40 books for children. He lives in Chapel Hill, NC.